W9-AFT-277

Picture the Past
Life in a
COLONIAL TOWN

Sally Senzell Isaacs

Heinemann Library
Chicago, Illinois

© 2001 Reed Educational & Professional Publishing
Published by Heinemann Library,
an imprint of Reed Educational & Professional Publishing,
Chicago, Illinois

Customer Service 888-454-2279
Visit our website at www.heinemannlibrary.com

Produced for Heinemann Library by
   Bender Richardson White.
Editor: Lionel Bender
Designer: Ben White
Picture Researcher: Cathy Stastny
Media Conversion and Typesetting: MW Graphics
Production Controller: Kim Richardson

04 03 02 01
10 9 8 7 6 5 4 3 2

Printed in Hong Kong

Library of Congress Cataloging-in-Publication Data.
Isaacs, Sally Senzell, 1950–
     Life in a colonial town / Sally Senzell Isaacs.
     p. cm. – (Picture the past)
     Includes bibliographical references and index.
     Summary: Reveals the lives of the people who set up the
first colonies in the United States, discussing their homes
and shelter, food, clothes, schools, communications, and
everyday activities.

ISBN 1-57572-312-3 (library binding)
1. United States-Social life and customs-To 1775-Juvenile
literature. 2. City and town life-United States-History-17th
century-Juvenile literature. 3. City and town life-United
States-History-18th century-Juvenile literature.
(1. United States-Social life and customs-To 1775. 2. City
and town life-History-17th century. 3. City and town life-
History-18th century.) I. Title.

E162.I83 2000
973.2-dc21
                                        99-089884

Special thanks to Mike Carpenter, Scott Westerfield, and
Tristan Boyer Binns at Heinemann Library for editorial and
design guidance and direction.

Acknowledgments
The producers and publishers are grateful to the
following for permission to reproduce copyright material:
Corbis: Corbis, page 6; Dave G. Houser, pages 1, 13, 14;
Richard T. Nowitz, pages 9, 17, 25; Annie Griffiths Belt,
pages 12, 16, 27; Nik Wheeler, page 15; Kelly-Mooney
Photography, pages 19, 28. Mary Evans Picture Library,
page 24. Peter Newark's American Pictures, pages 10,
20, 23. North Wind Pictures, pages 11, 18, 21.
Cover photograph: Corbis/Nik Wheeler.

Every effort has been made to contact copyright holders
of any material reproduced in this book. Omissions will
be rectified in subsequent printings if notice is given to
the publisher.

Illustrations by James Field, pages 22, 29; John James,
pages 8, 13, 26, 27; Nick Hewetson, page 7.
Map by Stefan Chabluk.
Cover make-up: Mike Pilley, Pelican Graphics.

Note to the Reader
Some words are shown in bold, **like this**.
You can find out what they mean by looking in the
glossary.

ABOUT THIS BOOK

This book is about daily life in the American colonies. The first of these colonies belonged to England, France, Spain, Holland, and Sweden. The book mostly describes English colonies during the years 1650 to 1750. We have illustrated the book with paintings and drawings from those times and with artists' ideas of how things looked then. We also include modern photographs of people dressed as colonists and of buildings that remain from colonial times.

The Consultant

Special thanks go to Diane Smolinski for her help in the preparation of this series. Diane Smolinski has years of experience interpreting standards documents and putting them into practice.

The Author

Sally Senzell Isaacs is a professional writer and editor of nonfiction books for children. She graduated from Indiana University, earning a B.S. degree in Education with majors in American History and Sociology. For some years, she was the Editorial Director of Reader's Digest Educational Division. Sally Senzell Isaacs lives in New Jersey with her husband and two children.

CONTENTS

Colonial Times

A colony is like a small, new village or town. It is created in a country by people from a foreign, or different, country. Beginning about 400 years ago, people from Europe started coming to America to start colonies. When people from France started a colony, the colony belonged to France. When people from England started a colony, the colony belonged to England. This book talks mostly about English colonies. It is based on historic Williamsburg, Virginia, one of the first colonial towns.

Look for these
The illustration of a colonist boy and girl sits alongside the title of each double-page story in the book.

The picture of a small colonial house marks boxes with interesting facts about colonial life.

TIMELINE OF EVENTS IN COLONIAL AMERICA

1492 Christopher Columbus lands near the coast of Florida.

1565 Spain starts the first permanent colony in St. Augustine, Florida.

1607 England starts its first permanent colony in Jamestown, Virginia.

1620 Europeans arrive in Plymouth, Massachusetts, on the *Mayflower.*

1500   1550   1600   1650

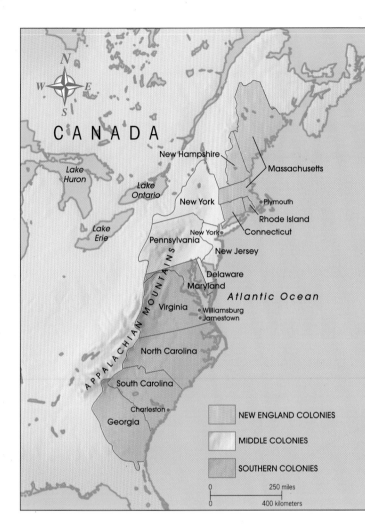

By 1750, England owned 13 colonies in North America. They were along or near the **coast** of the Atlantic Ocean. England's first lasting colony started in Jamestown, Virginia, in 1607.

1653 There are ten English colonies in America.

1682 French people begin settling around the Great Lakes, Missouri, and Mississippi Rivers.

1776 Thirteen colonies break from England and become the United States of America.

1650   1700   1750   1800

Starting a Colony

In the 1600s, it took two months to sail across the Atlantic Ocean from England to the North American colonies. It was a difficult trip. When the travelers arrived, they had plenty of work to do. They had to build houses. They had to plant seeds so they would have food to eat. These people who came to start a colony were called colonists.

People built their colonies near the place they landed and where it was easy to catch fish to eat. Ships brought cloth, animals, mail, and new colonists over from Europe. The ships carried corn, tobacco, fur, and lumber back to Europe.

A MAP of
the most INHABITED part of
VIRGINIA
containing the whole PROVINCE of
MARYLAND
with Part of
PENSILVANIA, NEW JERSEY AND NORTH CAROLINA
Drawn by
Joshua Fry & Peter Jefferson
in 1751.

Many colonists built their houses near each other. They built a **meetinghouse** close by. People used the meetinghouse for church services, parties, and meetings. Sometimes they used it as a school.

This is a 1680s colonial village. In the center is an area of open land where people let their horses and cattle eat.

IN THE VILLAGE

Look for:
1. Family houses
2. Meetinghouse
3. Land for animals
4. Cornmill with waterwheel
5. Blacksmith's workshop
6. Outside toilets

A Growing Town

Colonists wrote letters to their friends in Europe. "Come to America. Life here is good," they said. As more people arrived, small colonies grew into busy towns. **Craftspeople** opened stores. They made shoes, tools, silverware, wagon wheels, and barrels. Some towns had a post office where people could pick up mail and buy books and newspapers.

This is a colonial silversmith's shop. A silversmith can melt silver coins to make fancy bowls and pitchers.

NO MONEY

Usually colonists did not use money. They often paid for things by trading tobacco or corn.
If a carpenter needed a pair of shoes, he paid the shoemaker by making him a chair.

One of the town's busiest stores was called an **apothecary**. It sold medicine, tobacco, spices, and candy. People also went to the apothecary to buy eyeglasses and to get bad teeth pulled.

Many towns had a **tavern**. Travelers stopped at the tavern to eat and rest for the night. A traveler had to share a room with one or more strangers.

9

Spreading the News

Colonists heard most of their news from the town crier. He walked through the town ringing a bell. When people stopped to listen, he shouted out the news.

In this painting, publisher and inventor Benjamin Franklin checks the printing of the *Pennsylvania Gazette* newspaper in 1729.

Mail was delivered by a stagecoach or by a **post rider** on horseback. There were no stamps on letters. People paid the postage when they received their mail.

There were a few newspapers in the colonies. People read them to learn what was happening in Europe and other colonies. The papers came out only once a week. Newspapers had **advertisements** for such products as hats. They also advertised rewards for lost animals and runaway **slaves**.

SEALED WITH WAX

There were no envelopes in colonial days. People wrote a letter, folded over the paper, and sealed it with melted wax.

Houses

Many colonists built wooden houses. The wood came from nearby forests. Most houses had a stone fireplace. Its fire heated the house. It also was used for cooking. There were no sinks or toilets in the house. The toilet was outside in a small building called a **necessary**. People kept chamber pots under their beds. They used these pots during the night so they would not have to walk to the outdoor toilet.

People carried water to the house from an outdoor **well**. They used a pitcher of cold water to wash themselves every day. They only took a bath a few times a year.

WOODEN CHAIRS

Most colonists made their own furniture. Most people had simple wooden chairs, tables, and benches. Wealthy people sometimes bought fancy furniture that was made in Europe.

This is a cutaway drawing of a colonial house in Massachusetts in about 1750.

A Busy Day

Colonists worked hard. They grew their own food and made their own furniture and plates. Some people, usually men, worked outdoors. Women worked at home. They made candles, butter, soap, and yarn. They cooked, sewed, and took care of the children.

In the town, the blacksmith made horseshoes and iron tools. The miller made flour. The cooper made barrels and buckets.

The wheelwright made and repaired wheels for stagecoaches, wagons, and carts. Most people traveled in horse-drawn wagons.

Some colonists owned **slaves**. Many slaves worked on large farms called **plantations**. They were never paid for their work.

Slaves were not allowed to leave the plantations. They were not allowed to learn to read or write. They had no freedom. Some people were kind to their slaves. Others were very cruel to them.

Many slaves worked outside the houses. They grew crops, built barns and fences, and carried water buckets from the **well**.

A Child's Day

Children always had work to do. They woke early to milk the cows, gather eggs, and feed the chickens. Not all children went to school, but all children learned lessons from their parents. Boys learned to build, hunt, and fish. Girls learned to cook, sew, and spin thread.

Girls helped their mothers gather food from the fields and cook meals for all the family.

Children still had time to play games, such as throwing horseshoe-like quoits over wooden pegs on the ground.

Some boys, as young as ten years old, became **apprentices**. They learned a job by helping a **craftsperson**. Some apprentices learned to make tools from the blacksmith. Some learned to bake bread from the baker or make wheels from the wheelwright. Others worked with a printer and learned to print newspapers.

GAMES TO PLAY

Some games from colonial times are still popular today.
- Walking on stilts
- Ring toss
- Sack races
- Flying kites
- Marbles
- Bowling
- Blind Man's Bluff
- Spinning a top

Going to School

Some parents paid a teacher to give their children lessons at home. Other children went to a small one-room school. Schools were not free. Parents sent money or food to pay the teacher.

Children of all ages sat on benches in the same room. Younger children sat in front. Older children sat in back. Children who behaved badly sat in a corner or received a whipping.

Teachers were strict, but still the schoolroom was a noisy place. Some children read aloud while others practiced writing.

In winter, the chilly classroom was heated by a fireplace. Each child had to bring a piece of wood for the fire every day. Children who forgot had to sit far from the fire.

Some parents paid a traveling teacher to give music or dancing lessons.

School Lessons

Children learned to read, write, and solve math problems. There were no blackboards for the teachers to write on. There were no pencils. Many schools had no paper. Children read from the Bible and from a book called a **primer**. Sometimes they wrote on a flat piece of tree bark with a feather pen or a lump of coal.

The *New England Primer* of 1727 used rhymes to teach the alphabet.

NO BOOKS

Young children learned from a hornbook. It was like a wooden paddle. A piece of clear animal horn covered a sheet of paper. A hornbook was held in the hand.

A   In Adam's Fall
     We sinned all.

B   Thy Life to mend;
     This Book attend.

C   The Cat doth play,
     And after slay.

D   A Dog will bite
     A Thief at night.

E   An Eagle's flight
     Is out of sight.

F   The idle Fool
     Is whipt at school.

NO RULES

People spelled the same words different ways. There was no American dictionary yet. Some people spelled *music musick*. Some spelled *writing writeing*.

Most girls left school after they learned to read and write a little. They stayed home to help cook, clean, and make clothes. Some boys left school to work before they were twelve years old. Others went to high school or college and learned geography and the Latin language.

England helped set up colleges in its colonies, like this one in Williamsburg.

Clothes and Shoes

Clothes were expensive and took time to make. Most people had just two outfits. Girls and women always wore long dresses that covered their ankles and elbows. At home, they wore aprons to keep their dresses clean. They always wore hats on their heads, even at home.

Clothing was heavy and not comfortable. Most people made their own clothes. They wore leather or wooden shoes.

Many men and boys did not wear long pants. They wore knee-length pants called **breeches**. When they were not outdoors in cold weather, they wore long, woolen stockings. Zippers were not invented yet. The pants had buttons instead. Men and boys wore vests and jackets.

Wealthy people sometimes bought clothes and shoes from Europe.

Older boys in rich families dressed like their fathers.

Making Clothes

Many colonists wore woolen clothing. Wool comes from sheep. It took many steps to turn wool into dresses, pants, and jackets. First the wool is cut from the sheep. Then it is made into thread. Next the thread is woven into cloth. Last, the cloth is sewn into clothing.

BRIGHT COLORS

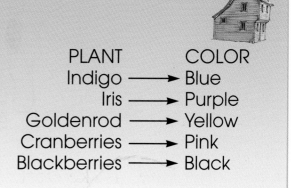

Children gathered plants. The plants were boiled in water with the wool until the wool turned color. Here are some of the plants and the colors they dyed wool.

PLANT	COLOR
Indigo ⟶	Blue
Iris ⟶	Purple
Goldenrod ⟶	Yellow
Cranberries ⟶	Pink
Blackberries ⟶	Black

Wool was cut from sheep using a large pair of scissors. This job is known as sheep shearing.

WIGS TO BUY

In big towns, most men and boys wore wigs. Wigs made of real hair cost the most money. Cheaper wigs were made of a mixture of goat and horse hair.

A wigmaker in Colonial Williamsburg shows how wigs were made.

Everyone helped make clothes. Grandmothers usually **carded** the wool by brushing it between two rough boards. This made the wool fluffy. Mothers and daughters put the wool on a spinning wheel to turn it into thread. Fathers and sons worked the **loom** to turn the thread into cloth. Mothers used needles and thread to sew the cloth into clothing.

What Colonists Ate

The first colonists grew most of their own food. They learned to grow corn, pumpkins, and squash from the local Native Americans. The Native Americans lived on the land before the colonists arrived.

Men hunted rabbits, squirrels, and deer. Near the sea, children fished and dug clams and **oysters** out of the sand.

In southern colonies, such as Virginia, the kitchen was outside the house. **Servants** carried the food to the dining room.

By 1748, farmers used wooden plows with iron blades. Horses or bulls pulled the plows through the fields.

People were afraid to drink water from the rivers. It was not clean and people got sick after drinking it. Instead, they drank **cider** made from apples. They also drank juice made from blueberries and cherries. Drinks were usually served from metal jugs into glass or leather mugs.

A DAILY MENU

BREAKFAST:
Cornmeal mush with maple syrup
NOON MEAL
(called dinner):
Stew made of meat and vegetables
SUPPER:
Another bowl of mush, but without the syrup

Cooking Food

Most food was cooked in the fireplace in the main room of the house. A pot hung down over the fire. Sometimes the pot had a stew of meat and vegetables. Sometimes it had a pudding made of eggs and sugar. Everyone had to be careful about burning their long clothes in the fire.

TO BEG A FIRE

It was important to keep the fire burning in the fireplace. If it went out, a child ran to the neighbor's house to get a hot coal from their fireplace to relight it.

Many fireplaces had ovens for baking bread, cookies, and pastries.

Colonial Recipe—Apple Pancakes

In the fall, colonists picked apples from their apple trees. They made apple pancakes on a flat, iron skillet that hung over the fire. Follow the instructions below to make apple pancakes as the colonists did.

WARNING: Do not cook anything unless there is an adult to help you. Always ask an adult to do the cutting and cooking on a hot stove.

YOU WILL NEED
- 1 1/2 cups (360 g) chopped apples
- 1/2 cup (120 g) flour
- 1/4 cup (60 g) sugar
- 2 eggs
- 3 tablespoons milk
- 1/2 cup (120 g) margarine or butter, melted
- 1 teaspoon cinnamon
- 1 pinch of salt

FOLLOW THE STEPS

1. Place all the ingredients in a bowl, except the apples.
2. Stir them together until you have a smooth mixture.
3. Stir in the chopped apples.
4. Pour the mixture onto a skillet or griddle and cook over a medium heat.
5. When the bottom of the pancake is brown, flip it over and brown the other side. Serve the pancake hot.

The Colonies Join

In 1776, leaders of the thirteen English colonies had a meeting. They decided to join together to form a new country, separate from England. In 1781, the colonies won a war against England. It is known as the War of **Independence** or the **Revolutionary** War. The colonies became the United States of America.

Leaders of the colonies met in Philadelphia. George Washington and John Adams —the first two presidents of the United States—were at the meeting.

Glossary

advertisement something in print that tries to sell a product or tell about an event

apothecary store that sells medicines, spices, and candy

apprentice someone who learns to do a job by working with a skilled craftsperson

breeches knee-length pants that fit tightly at the knee

card to comb wool between two small boards to prepare it for spinning

cider drink made by squeezing apples

coast land near a seashore

craftsperson someone skilled at making things with his or her hands

independence being free to do what one wants

loom machine used to weave thread into pieces of cloth

meetinghouse building where people get together for meetings, church services, and other events

necessary building outside a main house that has a toilet

oyster flat shellfish that lives in shallow water

plantation large farm where cotton, sugar, tobacco, or rice is grown

post rider someone who delivered the mail in the colonies

primer book used to teach young children to read

revolutionary bringing great change to how things are done or how a country is ruled

servant someone who works in another person's house, usually cooking, cleaning, and serving

slave person who is owned by another person and is usually made to work for that person

tavern place where travelers eat and sleep

well deep hole in the ground from which people get water

More Books to Read

Steen, Sandra, and Susan Steen *Colonial Williamsburg*. Morristown, N. J.: Silver Burdett Press, 1993.

Wroble, Lisa A. *Kids in Colonial Times*. New York: Rosen Publishing Group, 1997.

Index